When the Bow Breaks

Dr. Johnette Ruffner-Ceaser

Illustrations by Cameron Wilson

Liberated Expressions, LLC.
Laurel, Maryland

This is a work of fiction. Names, characters, places, and incidents either are the product of the author's imagination or are used fictitiously. Any resemblance to actual persons, living or dead, events, or locales is entirely coincidental.

Copyright © 2019 Dr. Johnette Ruffner-Ceaser

All Rights Reserved. No part of this book may be reproduced or used in any manner without written permission of the copyright owner except for the use of quotations in a book review.

Illustrations Copyright © 2019 by Cameron Wilson

ISBN 978-1-7337356-0-5 (paperback)
ISBN 978-1-7337356-1-2 (ebook)

Published by Liberated Expressions, LLC.
www.liberated-expressions.com

This book is for every woman, young and mature, who needs to know they are beautiful...naturally.

Hi, my name is Duckie. I am Pakina's favorite stuffed animal.

Pakina ("Puk Puk" is her nickname) and I have been together since she was one month old.

I know EVERYTHING about her.

I have so many stories to share, but today I want to tell you about the time her hairbow broke.

A broken hairbow may not seem like a big deal, but that bow changed our lives.

"Mom, why can't I get braids? There are only two girls in my class who don't have extensions!" said Pakina.

"Puk Puk, your hair is beautiful. It's long and thick. Most people would love to have your hair," said Mom.

With great frustration, Pakina uttered under her breath but just enough for Mom to hear, "Everybody else gets to do stuff except for me! I'm always left out."

"Doing stuff like everybody else" was a regular conversation between Pakina and her mom.

"Mom, why can't I get braids?"

"Why can't I get my hair flat ironed?"

"Why can't I get fake nails?"

"Why can't I get a cell phone?"

"Why can't I get on WeLook, SPYder or Flatter?"

The conversation always ended the same way, "Everybody else gets to do stuff except for me!"

Pakina was especially challenged by her mother's refusal to agree to a new hairdo. At the time, Pakina didn't understand that her mother was trying to help her to see her natural beauty and understand that she was a born leader who could encourage her friends to embrace their beauty, too.

Pakina's hair is like cotton candy. It is fluffy and soft like a down feather pillow, full like a bountiful garden, and it smells like the sweetest berries. Her eyes are shaped like almonds that twinkle with depth and dazzle with dreams.

Pakina's skin is rich and brown. The kind of brown that can only be found by the Nile, Congo or Zambezi Rivers. Her skin is smooth like stones that have been nurtured over time by the endless flow of water. She is almost as tall as her mother and well portioned like a star athlete.

She is an intellectual. As a two-year-old, even though she couldn't read, she memorized entire books. Her parents would deliberately skip parts of her favorites and she would kindly inform them of their mistake. At five years old she was having advanced conversations with her mother's friends, which left them in awe after every encounter.

At six years old, Pakina convinced her friends to start a business selling candy, slime, and jewelry at school. Pakina is also an inventor and a teacher. She is always repurposing recycled items to make new creations and she has a way with helping others to learn. She is Tinker Bell, a Disney princess, and Oprah Winfrey all wrapped in one.

God made Pakina absolutely awesome! She just doesn't realize it yet.

Pakina's hair was always styled in twists. Her mom was creative and had a knack for styling hair, so Pakina regularly wore cute styles that appealed to other girls and moms. Pakina wore short twists, wavy twists, curly twists, flat-twists, and more. You name it, Pakina had it!

Twists were a great option. They were trendy, versatile, convenient, and they kept Pakina's massive curls under control, which reduced the Hair Wash Day Battle.

"Mom, it hurts!"

"You're pulling my hair!"

"Are you done yet?"

"How much longer will it take?"

"My neck hurts. I can't hold my head down any longer!"

Without the twists, Pakina's hair looked like a 1,000 beautiful cotton balls. But if it rained or it was humid outside, those heavenly cotton balls transformed into hours of chaos and detangling.

In some ways, the twists disguised Pakina's hair. Unless you were present on wash day, no one knew about the majestic cotton balls. Even though Pakina and her mother saw the cotton balls regularly, I don't think they fully realized their significance.

Despite her mother's objection, Pakina surprisingly decided that she didn't want twists any longer. All she wanted was a single afro puff.

Her mom loved creating unique hair styles, but she reluctantly agreed to the boring, uneventful hairdo.

Pakina wore this style for weeks. Then suddenly the most amazing thing happened!

The bow, holding the puff in place, broke! It was like the cotton balls had a mind of their own and decided to break free.

"POW POW POOSH." It sounded like the popping of 10 balloons.

Her classmates, startled from the sound, looked up from their work in amazement.

There Pakina sat in the middle of the classroom surrounded by her glorious cotton balls.

"Pakina, you have an afro!" said one student.

Pakina sat sheepishly, only glancing at her classmates out of the corner of her eye. She wondered what they were thinking.

Before she could compose another thought, a chorus of 4th grade voices melodiously shared a soothing message.

"OMG, Pakina! Your hair is beautiful. I love it."

"Your hair is so thick and soft. How did you get it that way?"

"I want my hair like that!"

Amazed at the reaction of her classmates, Pakina soaked in the praise and for the first time embraced her beauty.

The next day, Pakina asked her mom if she could keep the afro. Her mom agreed and proceeded to apply moisturizer, detangle her hair, and round out the style to prevent the afro from looking like a "no-fro."

After the styling was complete, Pakina turned to look at her mom and for the first time her mom saw the cotton balls in a way that she had never seen them before.

"Puk Puk, you are stunning!"

She always felt that Pakina was beautiful, but today something was different.

Her mom took a picture and decided to post it on WeLook with this caption, "Despite other influences, she embraces her natural beauty. #afro #naturalbeauty.

Within a few hours, the post went viral!

People all over the world started to like and love Pakina's picture. They shared comments about how she has inspired them to embrace their natural beauty.

Ceaser
2 hrs

Despite other influences, she embraces her natural beauty. #afro #naturalbeauty.

👍 Like   💬 Comment   ➤ Share

 Write a comment...

Three days after the picture was posted, Pakina's mom received an IM from Congresswoman ZAIRE SA-LA-MA! Everyone thinks she will become the President one day.

She said, "I saw your daughter's picture on WeLook and I want to invite her to the next stop on my book tour. I want her to use my platform to inspire other young girls to love themselves, too."

Rep. Zaire Salama
15 min

I saw your picture on WeLook and I want to invite you to the next stop on my book tour. I want you to use my platform to inspire other young girls to love themselves, too.

Pakina was stunned! She didn't understand how her hair could create such a response and get the attention of ZAIRE SA-LA-MA!

Even though, Pakina couldn't understand what was happening. I, and her majestic cotton balls, understood. God placed us in Pakina's life to give her comfort when she needs it and to push her forward at the right time.

You see, the cotton balls broke the hair bow because it was time for Pakina to begin to recognize and embrace her natural beauty, so she can begin to bring forth her unique beauty into the world through her creativity, intellect, and ability to teach.

If she never learned how to love herself, she would never know how to love authentically and share her God-given gifts with others…naturally.

I don't know what God has in store for Pakina, but I can't wait to share the details with you.

Well, that's my story and I'm sticking to it!

See you next time!

Duckie

Made in the USA
Middletown, DE
17 June 2019